12.95

Copyright © 1986, Verlag Neugebauer Press, Salzburg–München.
Published in USA by Picture Book Studio USA,
an imprint of Neugebauer Press USA Inc.
Distributed by Alphabet Press, Natick, MA.
Distributed in Canada by Vanwell Publishing, St. Catharines, Ont.
Published in Great Britain by Neugebauer Press Publishing Ltd., London WC2.
Distributed in GB by Ragged Bears, Andover.

Printed in Austria by Druckhaus Nonntal, Salzburg.

LIBRARY OF CONGRESS CATALOGING IN PUBLICATION DATA

Kalas, Sybille.
The goose family book.

Translation of: Das Gänse-Kinder-Buch.
Summary: Text and photographs describe the physical characteristics
and behavior of a family of goslings from the moment they hatch
from eggs until they grow to adulthood.
1. Graylag goose — Behavior — Juvenile literature.
2. Familial behavior in animals — Juvenile literature.
[1. Graylag goose. 2. Geese] I. Title.
QL696.A52K3513   1986   598.4′1   85-30986
ISBN 0-88708-019-7   870261

Translated by Patricia Crampton.

Sybille Kalas

The Goose Family Book

Preface by Konrad Lorenz

PREFACE BY KONRAD LORENZ

*One of the most important and difficult tasks of modern educational science is to counteract the increasing alienation which is intruding between the modern and the "natural" world. What is nature? Our planet is populated by a great variety of complex organic systems, the harmony and beauty of which are increasingly forgotten by urbanized modern man. It may be wrong to draw conclusions for other people, but from my own childhood development I am convinced that the best remedy for man's total lack of understanding of natural harmony lies in giving children as much contact as possible with **live animals.** It is inherent in man's being that his sense of harmony with the natural world has to be awakened. For example, we understand instinctively the musical harmonies peculiar to our own culture; others must be learned.*

*So one cannot start too early when trying to put children in touch with the great harmonies. Since it is unfortunately impossible to make children go and live in the country, **books** are obviously among the most important educational tools for the modern town dweller. But a mere textbook is not enough; it must be a thing of **beauty,** that vividly brings home the beauty and harmony of nature and the natural system as a whole. The great variety of interaction between animals and plants as well as between animals themselves has to be brought to light, and the practical functions of beauty and harmony must be tellingly illustrated. The variety and beauty of unspoiled nature will then be seen as a reality; by contrast, the monotonous landscape of civilization will only sharpen this awareness.*

Nothing is more potent in opening a young person's eyes to nature than an emotional relationship with one animal, which can represent the whole of our living environment. But the child must always be told the truth about this animal; children have an uncommonly sharp ear for lies and if they ever catch you in one untruth, they will never trust you again. There is an old German pro-verb: "Lie once and never tell another lie: the world will call you liar till you die!'

Few people know one of the higher animals so well that a perceptive child will not spot some inaccuracy in their description. Few people know an untamed animal as well as Sybille Kalas knows the grey goose – and few are as dedicated as she is, both as an expert and as an artist. Moreover, few other animals have a social life so capable of inspiring the interest and sympathy of intelligent children. The delight in beauty which caused me to study geese scientifically is put to a different purpose in this book: to make people understand that other creatures on this earth besides human beings are capable of feeling and experiencing. This is an important realization, because it leads to a different view of man: a man who is not meant to rule over other life-forms like a hostile slave-owner, but is simply one of them; a man who, as a being endowed with reason, bears a responsibility for nature as a whole.

Imagine you are with us in a dew-drenched meadow, sparkling silver in the morning light of a late summer's day. Veils of mist rise from the wooded valleys as the sun sends its first rays over the mountains to the east. Far above you, where the sky is already bright with sunlight, flies a flock of wild geese. You hear their strident calls and answer them with a loud "Co-ome, co-ome." They are approaching fast, answering you, circling above the meadow, gliding down. Suddenly you are surrounded by wild geese, your ears full of their friendly cackling....

..And now you are going to make friends with the grey geese and find out why I live among them with my family, discovering how parent geese and goslings and their friends and acquaintances live together in the great flock.

My name is Sybille. Here you can see me swimming with my geese children,
Abel, Baker and Charlie. Like them, I have brought up a good many of our
geese — in other words, I have been a mother to them.
I have answered their quiet "bib-bib-bib" — "Here I am, where are you?", and
their loud crying sound: "Bee-bee-bee." I have carried them around under my
jersey to keep them warm when they were cold and tired.
I have taken them to good grazing ground and gone swimming with them.
In other words, I have done everything that good goose parents do!
That is why, now that all my geese children are grown up, I am allowed to live
with the flock as if I were one of them.

This is Jacob, my little boy.
He is growing up with the flock of geese and he likes to play where they are,
among his many grey-feathered brothers and sisters.

Spring is on the way and it is time for the geese to lay their eggs.
Today we are going out on the lake in the rowing-boat to look for nests.
Would you like to come?

We find the first nest on an island, well-hidden among the dry reeds.
The mother goose is standing beside the nest, otherwise we would never have found it. We think she may have come to lay an egg.
Because we are good friends with the geese, they allow us to go right up to their nests and even to touch the eggs. They would defend the nest furiously against strangers, or else take fright and fly away, never to return to their eggs.

There are four big eggs in the nest. They are quite cold and their shells feel rough, which tells us that the goose is not yet sitting on the eggs to hatch them out. When she begins to sit, her feathers will polish the eggs to a shiny yellow-brown.

In another nest we find six eggs. The goose has plucked a lot of soft, downy feathers from her breast and belly to line the nest.
That means she will soon begin to sit.

One day she will stay on the nest, ruffling up her thick belly feathers to cover her eggs like a soft, warm eiderdown.
They will take a whole month to hatch, but she is not going to sit there doing nothing all that time.
Even now she has to take good care of the babies growing up inside the eggs.

Above all she must always be on the alert, because ravens and crows like eggs to eat, and a fox can easily spot a careless goose.

Of course, the mother goose also has to eat, drink and bathe, so she leaves the nest for a short time every day, after covering the eggs with dry grass and feathers.
During this short break the pairs of geese often come to see us, knowing that we always have some grain for them.

When the goose returns to her nest she stands over the eggs and cleans them. Drops of water fall from her feathers, cooling and moistening the eggs. This keeps them "aired" which is very important for the goslings developing inside.

In order to grow, the embryo, which is the name we give to a living creature before it is born, actually needs air as well as the food it gets from the egg-yolk and white. The egg "breathes" through minute pores in the shell, under which there is a fine network of veins. The blood in the veins carries the fresh air to the embryo and the used air back to the eggshell and out again.
Then the goose settles herself very slowly and carefully, tucking grass, reeds and feathers firmly around her with her beak so that none of the precious heat is lost.

This is Cinders. Small green leaves are already showing on the tree above her nest, and fresh, soft grass is sprouting up around it, providing the best possible food for the goslings. The sun shines for a little longer every day.
Everything is ready for Cinders' children, which will very soon hatch out.
She lets me feel under her belly, in the dark, warm hollow of her nest, and carefully remove one egg.

If you hold an egg at the end of a rolled-up newspaper and look through it at the sun you can see how the goslings have developed. Yes, we can clearly see them moving now inside the eggs!
It won't be long before they hatch and we are already looking forward to seeing Cinders' goose babies.

Jacob holds an egg to his ear, and what does he hear?
From inside the egg comes a very soft "Bib-bib, bib-bib-bib!"
Did you know that goslings talk to each other while they are still in the egg?
They are telling each other when they are ready to hatch, so that they all
come out at almost the same time.
And when they cry inside the egg they are telling their mother that they feel
cold.Then she turns the eggs around and says a calm and comforting
"gag-gag-gag" to her children. When she hears their soft "bib-bib-bib" in reply
she knows they are all right.
We return the egg to the nest and leave the island, because Cinders and
her hatching babies need rest. As we row back we can see Blaze, Cinders'
husband, keeping watch near the nest. We shall come back tomorrow
morning and then we shall see what we shall see…

Tonight the goslings will hatch out under Cinders' warm belly.

First each gosling cracks a little hole in the shell, which is now yellow-brown and gleams like silk, polished by the mother goose's feathers.

Bit by bit the gosling opens up a crack all round the shell until there is room for it to squeeze out.

The gosling is too tired to lift its head after all that hard work.

Its little feathers are still enclosed in thin cases of horn which will fall off later. Just now, they make the gosling look quite wet.

As soon as the horn cases have fallen off its feathers, the baby goose looks like a fresh tuft of pussy-willow.

At the tip of its shiny black beak you can still see the yellow egg-tooth the gosling used to crack open its shell. Soon this too will fall away.

Early next morning we go to visit Cinders. Blaze is swimming close to the nest now and he hisses furiously at us. Now that his babies have hatched out he does not want us anywhere near. But Cinders sits quietly on her nest, her feathers fluffed out, listening to the clear, piping voices of the goslings telling their mother how good they feel.

There they are, peeping out from under Cinders' lifted wing: the still damp, yellow-green chicks with their bright, alert dark eyes. "Bib-bib," they pipe, and Cinders answers with tender, breathy sounds.

One more day, and the goslings will "blossom" into those pussy-willow tufts. Then their parents will lead them away from the nest to swim in some, safe, hidden inlet. Blaze will stand guard while Cinders lies down near her babies, ready to take them back under her warm feathers at any moment.

Next day the goose family comes swimming towards us. You can see how well Mother Cinders and Father Blaze watch over their three children.

It's almost impossible to believe that the goslings hatched out of their eggs only yesterday.
And a month before that there was nothing inside the eggs but egg-white and a yolk with a tiny round disc on it. Thanks to the warmth of the mother goose's belly, this tiny speck, called the germinal disc, has now grown into a dear little gosling which looks at you and talks to you and enjoys your visits!

The goslings learn a great deal in the first days of their life, such as choosing the grasses and plants which taste good.

They also meet other goose families and learn to tell them apart from their own family.

Although they are only a few days old, and very small and soft, the goslings have fights with each other.

They attack with wide-open beaks, biting each others faces and necks and tugging and tweaking at the downy feathers. They even try to beat at each other with their wings, just like adult geese in a fight. But their little wings are so short, they simply flap in the air.

In this and many other ways the gosling family get to know each other and soon each gosling knows which brother or sister is going to boss him around and which ones he can boss, when they are grazing or dabbling or settling down to sleep.

Once they have worked out the ranking order among themselves, the gosling family have no more quarrels. Instead they always greet each other with outstretched necks, a clear "bibibibibibib."

It is extremely important for a goose family to get along well together without quarrelling, because the babies must not lose touch with their own family. Without the protection and warmth of the big geese they would not survive a single night, and that is why the chicks follow so closely in their parents' footsteps.

As soon as the little geese are tired or cold they tell their mother all about it with their piping "sleep sounds." Then Cinders settles down and lets the babies creep under her wings.
This little fellow has had his sleep and is coming out to cackle cheerfully to his mother.

As the children grow bigger there is not much room under their mother's wings. When they have snuggled their little behinds into the warm, out pop their heads again. It's useful to be able to use Cinders' shoulder feathers for a roof!

The geese are growing up fast.
Their legs grow first, because for the long distances they have to walk and
swim with the parent geese they need strong legs and webbed feet which
look much too big for the soft little chicks.

After about a month the fluffy ball of "pussy-willow" has already grown into
a proper little rascal. This is Nick.
He has nice smooth belly feathers now, but there is still some baby down left
on his head and neck.
The strong flight feathers are already growing from blue quills on his wings.

Before the geese are two months old they are wearing a beautiful sleek coat of feathers and soon their powerful pinions will carry them high into the air.

Those babies, so much in need of protection, have grown into strong, self-assured birds who know all about the position their family occupies in the flock and insist on their rights, cackling away alongside their parents.

Now they too are flying!
Cautiously at first, and for short distances…

…but soon they soar up with their parents into the blue summer sky and join together with other families in the wedge formation common to all wild geese.

Will they ever come back again?
Jacob looks a little doubtful as he watches them, but…

…of course they will!
   Calling loudly, down they fly, turning over on their backs to help them drop all
   the faster —
   now they are gliding, their wings curved in a graceful arch —
   scarcely higher than the highest trees —

and coming in to land with a clatter of wing-beats, the wind of their flight blowing round our ears, their pink legs stretched forward.

And here they come now,
very close to us,
and as friendly and confident as if they had never been wild geese flying far away, high above the mountaintops.